POLLINATORS

LYN SIROTA

Rourke
Educational Media

rourkeeducationalmedia.com

Scan for Related Titles
and Teacher Resources

Before Reading:

Building Academic Vocabulary and Background Knowledge

Before reading a book, it is important to tap into what your child or students already know about the topic. This will help them develop their vocabulary, increase their reading comprehension, and make connections across the curriculum.

1. *Look at the cover of the book. What will this book be about?*
2. *What do you already know about the topic?*
3. *Let's study the Table of Contents. What will you learn about in the book's chapters?*
4. *What would you like to learn about this topic? Do you think you might learn about it from this book? Why or why not?*
5. *Use a reading journal to write about your knowledge of this topic. Record what you already know about the topic and what you hope to learn about the topic.*
6. *Read the book.*
7. *In your reading journal, record what you learned about the topic and your response to the book.*
8. *After reading the book complete the activities below.*

Content Area Vocabulary
Use glossary words in a sentence.

adaptations

anther

biodiversity

compound

ecology

folate

metamorphosis

neonicotinoids

physiology

prehensile

stigma

After Reading:

Comprehension and Extension Activity

After reading the book, work on the following questions with your child or students in order to check their level of reading comprehension and content mastery.

1. *Why do bees prefer to eat pesticide-contaminated food? (Summarize)*
2. *Name the four cycles of life an insect goes through. (Infer)*
3. *How many species of bumblebees are there in the United States? (Asking questions)*
4. *Butterflies and moths have "compound eyes." Describe what this means. (Text to self connection)*
5. *Besides humans, who is the largest known pollinator? (Asking questions)*

Extension Activity

The cycle of life! The book describes the four cycles of life an insect goes through. Using poster board and markers, construct a diagram of each cycle by drawing what the insect looks like at each stage of development. Add some interesting facts about what goes on during each stage.

TABLE OF CONTENTS

POLLINATORS AND POLLINATION

Nearly all the food we eat is made possible by pollinators. The human race cannot survive without them. Eighty percent of the world's 1,400 crop plants depend on visits from pollinators. In the United States, the pollination of crops is valued at 10 billion dollars per year!

4

Entomologists are scientists who study insects. They focus on life cycle, habitat distribution, **physiology**, behavior, **ecology**, and the population of insects. Anthecologists, or pollination biologists, study the process of pollination and relationships between flowers and pollinators. Plants and pollinators have developed their close relationships for millions of years.

5

Pollination is the process of moving pollen grains from the male **anther** part of a flower to the female **stigma** part of a flower. While it can happen naturally through wind or water, it's often due to insects, birds, and small mammals.

pollen grains

Insects pollinate when they visit flowers containing pollen, a sticky, yellowish substance. Many insects have pollen-trapping hairs on their bodies or pollen baskets on their hind legs. They transfer pollen while visiting their food source, called biotic pollination. Once pollinated, seeds grow!

Flying insects such as bees and butterflies are common pollinators. They are most successful at transferring pollen. Wasps pollinate, but lack the body hair to be as effective as honeybees.

Beetles were prehistoric pollinators who visited plants 150 million years ago. They pollinate in the process of eating plants rather than sipping nectar. Moths and flies pollinate too. Flies pollinate more than 100 crops. Others are mosquitos, midges, and ants.

Lesser long-nosed bats

Besides humans, the largest known pollinator is the black and white ruffed lemur. In Madagascar, they use their flexible hands, long noses, and tongues to dig deep inside flowers. They collect pollen on their faces and fur that they transfer.

ENDANGERED POLLINATORS

In the United States at least:
3 bat species
5 bird species
24 butterfly, skipper, and moth species
1 beetle and fly species
are federally listed as endangered under the Endangered Species Act of 1973.

Tropical mammals such as bats, bush babies, and sugar gliders pollinate. Lizards, geckos, and skinks climb inside flowers to drink nectar and end up with coated scales! Birds are pollinators too.

Australia's honey possum has **adaptations** that assist pollination. Grasping feet and a **prehensile** tail allow it to hang and move pollen.

Without pollinating midges, we would not have chocolate. Midges pollinate the tiny white flowers of the cacao tree, allowing it to produce fruit.

Scientists that study butterfly and moth pollinators are called lepidopterists. They use scanning electron microscopes and DNA sequencing to understand the biology and relationships.

A DAY IN THE LIFE

Insects all go through four stages of a life cycle: egg, larva, pupa, and adult. This cycle is a total **metamorphosis**. They grow by molting, shedding their old exoskeleton and growing a new one.

Insects are attracted to flowers based upon attributes like color, scent, shape, and size. For example, the corpse flower smells like a dead, rotting animal in order to attract flies.

Moths work the night shift. Some orchids are pollinated by moths. As orchids have changed or evolved, their relationship with moths have too! Certain orchids have gotten longer. Moths have adaptively stretched their tongues to reach the nectar of these orchids.

Butterflies and moths have **compound** eyes that see wide views. They sense motion well and see more colors than humans, assisting pollination practices. Taste receptors on their feet and on the tip of the proboscis, or drinking straw, help them drink nectar. Bristles on their legs carry pollen.

Female worker bees are responsible for gathering pollen and nectar for the bee colony.

The Western honeybee is responsible for one in three mouthfuls of food you eat! With ultraviolet vision, honeybees see which flowers are filled with nectar. Two stomachs are doubly delicious for digestion and storing nectar for honey! Other beneficial bee products are wax, pollen, royal jelly, and glue.

Pollinators like bees perform a waggle dance. The dance means, "Here's where to find the food!" Scientists have found bees and plants communicate through electric signals. Tests show bees distinguish between floral fields. Electric signals may also let insects know a flower has already been visited.

Most bees dig nests in soil. Others create holes in plant stems or wood. Some use holes made by other insects. Honeybees may nest in tree hollows. They line nest cells with a waxy material they make.

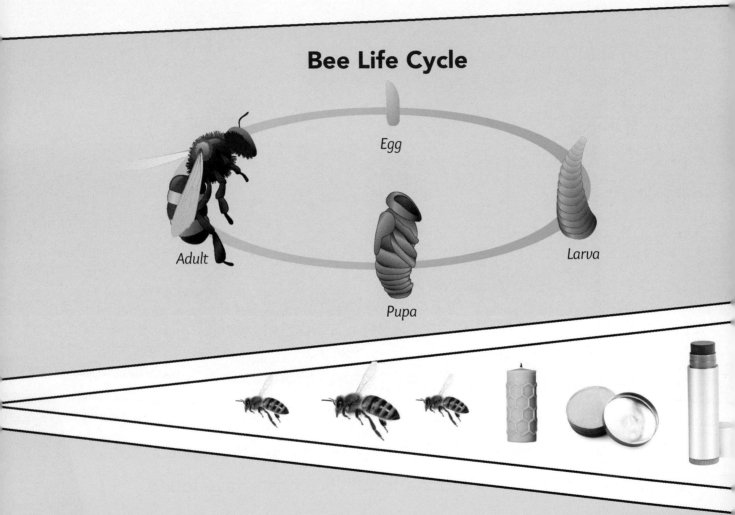

Bee Life Cycle

Egg

Larva

Pupa

Adult

In 1862, a British orchid grower sent Charles Darwin a series of orchids from Madagascar. Darwin predicted the existence of an unknown insect species based on flower size and his understanding of the evolution of orchids and insects. In 1907, his prediction was proven. In 1992, observations showed the moth feeding on the flower and transferring pollen. This is further evidence of Darwin's theory of natural selection.

POLLINATION DOMINATION

In addition to benefiting humans, pollination is vital to the life cycle of plants. It helps them produce fruit or seeds. There are two methods of pollination: self pollination and cross pollination. Cross pollination is most common.

Bees have been noted as the main pollinators. Sometimes, however, bees act as thieves by taking pollen without providing pollination.

There are 49 species of bumblebees in the United States. They are important pollinators for wildflowers. Bumblebees make high frequency vibrations, called buzz pollination, to free up pollen.

Pollinating insects are critical for increasing crops. They support **biodiversity.** There is a relationship between plant and pollinator diversity.

Pollinators can be exposed to pesticides in floral nectar and pollen. Some studies have shown that **neonicotinoids** have negative effects on bees and colonies.

Populations of bees and other insect pollinators have fallen dramatically in recent years. Scientific evidence suggests pesticides may be to blame.

Further research indicates bees prefer to eat pesticide-contaminated food. Neonicotinoids affect the brains of bees in similar ways that nicotine affects human brains. This "drug" laced food keeps luring bees back for more, fueling addictive behavior.

Worldwide about 1,000 plants grown for food, drink, fibers, spices, and medicine need to be pollinated to produce important consumer products. Some of these are: apples, blueberries, coffee, melons, peaches, cotton, potatoes, pumpkins, vanilla, and almonds. More than half the world's diet of fats and oils come from pollinated plants.

Pollinators support crops that make essential nutrients for malnourished regions of the world. Scientists have found three of the most essential nutrients are vitamin A, iron, and **folate**. Less developed regions of the world such as India, South Asia, and sub-Saharan Africa depend on natural pollinators for crops that produce these nutrients.

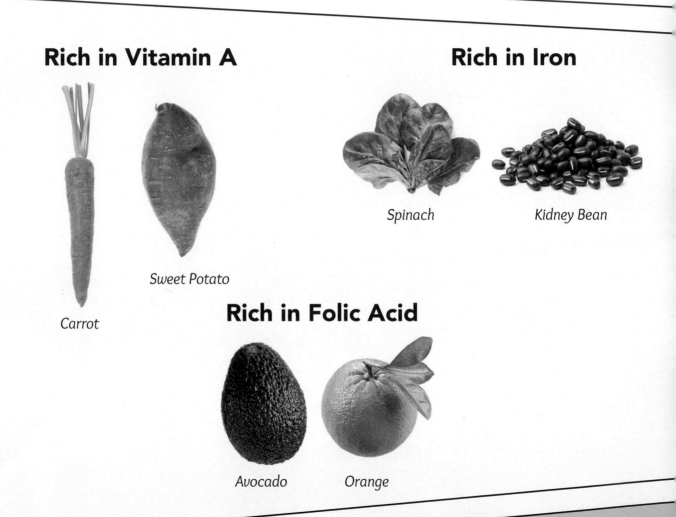

Rich in Vitamin A

Carrot

Sweet Potato

Rich in Iron

Spinach

Kidney Bean

Rich in Folic Acid

Avocado

Orange

The link between global nutrition and pollinators makes further research into the decline of pollinator populations critical.

Poorer regions that are more dependent on pollinators need to adjust. They must work with managed bee colonies to supplement wild pollinators. They can also shift to crops, similar in nutrients, that don't depend on pollination. Importing nutrient-rich foods from other regions is also helpful in moving these regions into balance.

Broccoli and cauliflower do not need pollinators.

MAKE WAY FOR ROBOBEES

Harvard University researchers have introduced the first robobees. They are bee-sized robots with the ability to lift off the ground and hover in mid-air with a power supply. Their super thin robot wings can flap 120 times per second! It is believed that within the next few years they will artificially pollinate a field of crops.

WHAT'S BUGGING BEES?

Over the past century, many forests have shifted from open to closed canopies. The canopy holds the upper forest or habitat zone. This change in forest structure may be contributing to pollinator decline. Bees are less common when shrubbery is dense.

24

INTERE-STING

A bee stinger has different toxins, or bee venom, than that of a wasp. So a person who has an allergy to wasp stings may not suffer from a bee sting allergy. Honeybees will die if they sting humans, but can sting predators repeatedly. Bumblebees have a smooth stinger and are able to sting repeatedly, but are rarely aggressive.

The North American Pollinator Protection Campaign (NAPPC) is a group studying honeybee health. They published a comprehensive list of stressors including: parasitic mites, microscopic fungus, viruses, bacterial diseases, pesticides, nutrition, genetics, queen quality, and the proper management of honeybee colonies.

Scientists use the term colony-collapse disorder (CCD) to represent the drastic change in the bee population.

In 2006, commercial beekeepers started noticing that honeybees were disappearing. In 2013, one-third of U.S. honeybee colonies died or disappeared during the winter. This is a 42 percent increase of loss over the prior year.

The United States has slowly become a poor host to honeybees. To survive, they need to forage for food. Open spaces and places for bees to do this have become scarce. Countrysides have become factory fields of corn and soybean, which is like a desert for bees.

Habitat loss and climate change affect all pollinators. Air and water pollution are as toxic to pollinators as they are to humans.

There are steps you can take to help pollinators. Plant native plants in your yard that are different shapes and colors. Add milkweed for monarch butterflies. Leave some of the ground bare for bee nesting.

Ensure plantings bloom in spring for bumblebee queens, to help them start colonies. Go easy on chemicals. Instead use plants that draw natural pest-eaters.

CREATE A POLLINATOR HANG OUT FROM RECYCLED PLASTIC

Supplies Needed:

clean, empty plastic two-liter (.002 cubic meter) bottles
scissors
stapler
hole punch
long strand of twine
items for the hang-out space: twigs, leaves,
  bark, pine cones, straws,
mesh produce bag

Directions

1. Make space. To create hang out compartments, cut the bottom five inches (12.7 centimeters) off each bottle. Have an adult assist. Staple the bottle bottoms together so the hang out is cozy.

2. Hang it. Punch two holes an inch (2.54 centimeters) apart in each cup. Pull twine through holes until it's wrapped all the way around the cups. Tie the ends of the twine in a knot at the top.

3. Put all items, such as the twigs, into each compartment. Some compartments can be covered with the mesh bag to prevent loose items from falling out.

Bee Holey: Non-stinging bees love holes. With help from an adult, drill holes into a block of wood and add to the hang out. Make sure the wood is not pressure-treated with chemicals.

GLOSSARY

adaptations (ad-ap-tay-shuhns): changes that a living thing goes through so it fits in better with its environment

anther (an-thur): the part of a flower at the tip of the stamen that contains its pollen

biodiversity (bye-oh-duh-vur-si-tee): the condition of nature in which a wide variety of species live in a single area

compound (kahm-pound): a substance, such as salt or water, made from two or more chemical elements

ecology (i-kah-luh-jee): the scientific study of the relationships between living things and their environment

folate (fohl-ate): a vitamin B that is naturally present in many foods

metamorphosis (met-uh-mor-fuh-sis): a series of changes some animals, such as caterpillars, go through as they develop into adults

neonicotinoids (nee-oh-ni-coh-teen-oyds): chemicals used to eliminate insect pests

physiology (fiz-ey-ah-luh-jee): the branch of biology that deals with functions of living things and their parts

prehensile (pri-hen-sile): the ability to grab or hold

stigma (stig-ma): the tip of the pistil of a flower where pollen is received

INDEX

SHOW WHAT YOU KNOW

1. Describe colony collapse disorder. How does it affect pollinators?

2. List two examples of animal adaptations that have been beneficial to pollination.

3. What is biotic pollination? What is buzz pollination?

4. Describe how pollinators are critical to regions of the world that are not as developed as the United States.

5. Why do you think neonicotinoids are bad for pollinators? Compare the relationship to humans that become dependent on something.

WEBSITES TO VISIT

www.fs.fed.us/wildflowers/pollinators/documents/simpletruthbrochure.pdf

www.pollinator.org/education.htm

www.nrcs.usda.gov/wps/portal/nrcs/main/national/plantsanimals/pollinate

ABOUT THE AUTHOR

Lyn Sirota has written many science and nature books, articles, and poems for children. She spends her days writing, teaching/practicing yoga and volunteers in local schools and animal shelters. Lyn lives in central New Jersey with her husband, children and three furry rescues. For more information about her work visit: www.lynsirota.com and blog: http://blog.lynsirota.com.

© 2017 Rourke Educational Media

www.rourkeeducationalmedia.com

PHOTO CREDITS: Cover: ©Srabin, ©schnuddel, ©Steve Ellingson; p.01: ©Dr. John Brackenbury; p.03: ©GRACHEVA T O; p.04: ©Pacotoscano, ©Cornel Constantin; p.05: ©YURI_KRAVCHENKO, ©KirsanovV; p.06: ©paula french; p.07: ©Rafael Barbizan Sühs, ©JJ Harrison; p.08: ©Nerijus Sujeta, ©enviromantic; p.09: ©Appfind, ©Merlin D. Tuttle; p.10: ©fcafotodigital, ©fstop123; p.11: ©Sutisa Kangvansap; p.12: ©SIRA, ©JAFFAR ALI PHOTOGRAPHY; p.13: ©Pichamon S, ©nevenm; p.14: ©azur13; p.15: ©Panya Sealim; p.16: ©Antagain, ©AGEphotography, ©Skorobogatov Dmytro, ©HighImpactPhotography; p.17: ©njmcc; p.18: ©GREGORY DUBUS; p.19: ©TippaPatt; p.20: ©baona; p.21: ©Sjoerd van der Wal; p.22: ©Andrzej Tokarski, ©Photodsotiroff, ©pepifoto, ©ansonsaw, ©Anna Yu, ©Valentyn Volkov; p.23: ©sandsun; p.24: ©Nikada, ©Scott Camazine; p.25: ©Chet Chaimangkhalayon, ©Andrew Neil Dierks; p.26: ©Lazing Bee; p.27: ©DS70, ©Dmitry_7; p.28: ©Steve Debenport; p.29: ©David Freund

Edited by: Keli Sipperley
Cover design by: Tara Raymo www.creativelytara.com
Interior design by: Jen Thomas

Library of Congress PCN Data

Insects as Pollinators / Lyn Sirota
(Insects As …)
ISBN (hard cover)(alk. paper) 978-1-68191-693-4
ISBN (soft cover) 978-1-68191-794-8
ISBN (e-Book) 978-1-68191-892-1
Library of Congress Control Number: 2016932569

Also Available as:

Printed in the United States of America, North Mankato, Minnesota